HYPATIA

Ancient Alexandria's Female Scholar

BILLIE HOLLADAY SKELLEY

ILLUSTRATED BY
JAMES PAUL SKELLEY

THE CROSSING TIME SERIES – BOOK 4

Hypatia: Ancient Alexandria's Female Scholar
Copyright © Billie Holladay Skelley 2021
Copyright © Billie Holladay Skelley 2024
Paperback-Press (Kids Book Press) (2021)
Crossing Time Press (2024)
All Rights Reserved

ISBN-13: 978-1-959489-03-0
Library of Congress Control Number: 2021916732

PUBLISHER'S NOTE:
Without limiting the rights under the copyright reserved above, no part of this publication may be reproduced, stored in or introduced into a retrieval system, or transmitted, in any form or by any means (electronic, mechanical, photocopying, recording or otherwise), without the prior written permission of both the copyright owner and the publisher of this book.

Cover design and illustrations by James Paul Skelley
Manufactured in the United States of America

For
James

who shares the love of learning

TABLE OF CONTENTS

Chapter 1: A Curious Child 3

Chapter 2: A Devoted Student 9

Chapter 3: An Independent Spirit 15

Chapter 4: A Dedicated Teacher 19

Chapter 5: A Respected Philosopher 27

Chapter 6: An Unintended Martyr 35

Chapter 7: A Lasting Heroine 43

Vocabulary 46

Did You Know? 49

Source Notes 50

References 52

Chapter 1: A Curious Child

"Father, what are the names of these fish?"

"I will tell you all of their names, Hypatia."

"Will you teach me to swim so I can move through the water just as the fish do?"

"Yes, Hypatia."

"I should like to learn about horses, too, and how to ride them."

"I will teach you, Hypatia."

"Will you also teach me to drive a chariot?"

"Yes, Hypatia. You shall learn all these things and more."

Hypatia, an **inquisitive** and beautiful child, was born in the fourth century, sometime between 350-370 CE. It was so long ago historians are not certain of her exact date of birth, but they know she was born in the ancient city of Alexandria. This city was located in northern Egypt near where the Nile River intersects the Mediterranean Sea.

At that time, Alexandria was part of the Roman Empire, and it was a city with many different people, cultures, and religions. Recognized for its trade and **commerce**, the city was also noted for its arts and laws.

Alexandria was also a great center for learning. Students from distant lands came to study at the Alexandrian Museion (or Museum) and Library. The Museion was a temple honoring the Muses—the Greek goddesses of creativity in literature, science, and the arts—but it was also a place for acquiring and preserving knowledge.

The Museion had several different schools, lecture halls, reading rooms, and places to study. It also had a dining area, beautiful gardens, fountains, and tree-lined pathways. The Library is estimated to have held between 500,000 and 700,000 volumes on its shelves, and these handwritten scrolls included some of the most **scholarly** works in the world. Together the Alexandrian Museion and Library were like a modern university—a place where great minds could gather and exchange ideas. Another smaller, but famous library in Alexandria was located at the Temple of Serapis—the Greek-Egyptian god associated with **fertility**, healing, and the afterlife. This library was called the Serapeum. With its Museion and great libraries, the city of Alexandria was a remarkable place where many **scholars** came to study and learn.

Hypatia's father, Theon, was a member of the Alexandrian Museion. He was a mathematician and astronomer who spent much time studying the works of **Euclid** and **Ptolemy**. Theon was also a poet, teacher, and writer. Since he worked and studied at the Museion, Theon was able to raise his daughter, Hypatia, almost from the day she was born, in a very stimulating environment of learning and exploration.

Even when she was very young, Theon taught Hypatia many things other young girls at that time did not learn to do. He educated her as if she was his son instead of his daughter. Two very important things Theon taught Hypatia were how to read and to write, and Hypatia was exceptionally good at both. She was a very curious child who liked to explore the world in which she lived, and she thrived in the intellectual surroundings in which she was raised.

Chapter 2: A Devoted Student

"Father, will you teach me about numbers and how you use them in studying mathematics?"

"Yes, Hypatia. I will teach you."

"I see that the numbers have patterns. There is a logical nature to them."

"Yes, Hypatia, I believe you will come to love numbers."

Theon did teach his daughter about numbers, and he was right in his belief: Hypatia came to love numbers and mathematics. She began her study at first with simple problems in arithmetic, but soon she was mastering advanced principles in **geometry**. She learned about cones, spheres, and other geometric shapes. Numbers were very special to Hypatia because of their **abstract** nature, their logical rules, and their multiple uses. For her, the study of mathematics was an important and valuable part of a good education.

Theon also taught Hypatia about **astronomy**. She learned about the moon, planets, stars, and constellations. She observed how these heavenly bodies moved across the night sky, and she used mathematics to calculate their positions and to predict their movements. Hypatia also learned to predict eclipses.

Beyond astronomy, Hypatia also studied other sciences, literature, and poetry. She spent a great deal of time studying **grammar** and developing her speaking skills. She focused on the art of **rhetoric**—the ability to communicate well with the spoken word. She learned to use her voice in a gentle, pleasing, confident, and persuasive manner. Eventually, she was able to both inform and motivate people when she addressed them.

Hypatia also explored philosophy—the study of ideas regarding truth and knowledge, life and reality, and the meaning of existence. She debated various topics with other students, such as what causes an action to be considered good or evil. With other scholars, she discussed why some acts are regarded as right or wrong. She wanted to learn what values people considered important. For Hypatia, such topics were fascinating. She liked using logic to discover truths.

Beyond mathematics, astronomy, rhetoric, and philosophy, Hypatia also studied different religions. She learned about the Jewish faith, the Christian religion, and Paganism. Paganism was a term that covered many different beliefs and practices—from worshiping the old Greek, Roman, and Egyptian gods and goddesses to following different philosophies or non-Christian schools of thought. Hypatia studied different religions to learn about their various **doctrines** and beliefs.

Hypatia was extremely disciplined in her studies. With her sharp intellect and strong commitment to the hard work of learning, Hypatia explored many different areas and examined a variety of subjects. She wanted to be able to draw her own conclusions, to think independently, and to use scientific thought and reasoning to identify truths. Simply put, Hypatia was a devoted student who loved to learn.

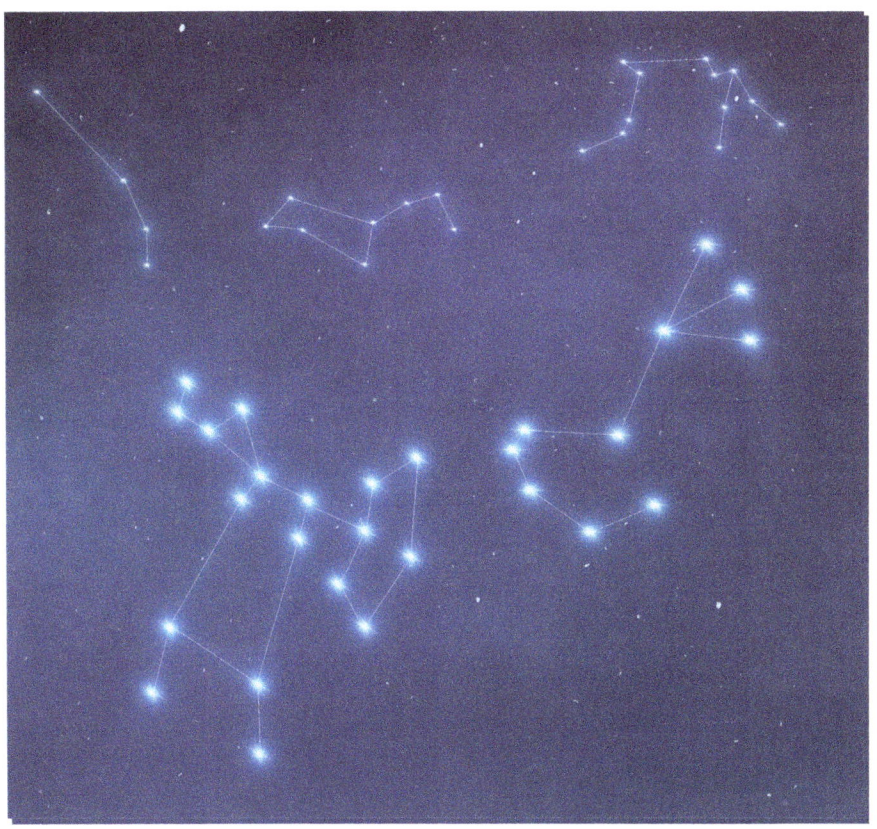

Chapter 3: An Independent Spirit

"Have you seen the woman called Hypatia?"

"Yes. She is certainly beautiful, but she doesn't act like any woman I know."

"I agree. I have seen her driving her own chariot about the city. It seems she hardly ever stays at home."

"Hypatia seems to move freely, going where she wants when she wants. She doesn't dress like a woman either."

"Yes, her clothing is simple and modest. She wears the tribon—the long, white academic robe of a scholar—just as a man would wear."

"Hypatia is different, but she does move with such grace and beauty. They say her voice is so **melodic** that everyone wants to hear her speak."

It is likely Hypatia did seem unusual to many women in Alexandria because, all in all, she was presenting a relatively new image of womanhood. Most young women, who were close to her age, were focusing on marriage and running a household, but Hypatia was becoming a scholar. Even though she had **suitors**, she chose not to marry and not to have children. Instead of spending her time at home preparing food and caring for a family, Hypatia traveled about the city focusing on learning and preserving knowledge.

Unlike many of the other women in Alexandria, Hypatia was not frightened at the prospect of entering into a group of men and exchanging ideas with them. She openly associated with other scholars, and she was becoming a respected **academic**. In addition, few women in Alexandria were known beyond their immediate family group and nearby neighbors, but Hypatia was becoming a well-known, prominent, public figure. Admired for her **purity** and **virtue**, she impressed people with her intelligence, dignified behavior, and social skills. Hypatia heard her own drummer, chose her own paths, and truly was an independent spirit.

Chapter 4: A Dedicated Teacher

"Hypatia, I regret that I must leave Alexandria and will no longer be able to hear your lectures and participate in your discussions. Your teaching has greatly inspired me, and I will not forget you."

"You are a good student, Synesius. I will miss you. I believe you will advance to positions of great power and wide influence."

As Hypatia's knowledge and expertise grew, she became a teacher. She taught mathematics, astronomy, and philosophy. Attracted at first by her charm, **charisma**, and personal presence, Hypatia's students soon were impressed by her brilliant mind. They were often awed by her powers of reasoning. Hypatia's students respected her teaching efforts because she made difficult subjects easier for them to understand. She was devoted to her students and earned their admiration with her intelligence and dedication.

Recognized for her pleasing voice, Hypatia also became very popular as a lecturer. She often conducted her lectures in the form of a dialogue or discussion, and her pupils enjoyed the interactions. They respected and admired her persuasive skills as a speaker. Hypatia's lectures often **exhilarated** and inspired her students so much that her influence still affected many of them long after they left her classes.

As word of her brilliance as a teacher and her skills as a lecturer spread, students from all across the ancient world came to study and learn from Hypatia. Drawn primarily from the wealthy and **elite** classes, many of her students came from different cultures and different religious backgrounds—including Christian and non-Christian faiths. Hypatia taught them all. It did not matter to Hypatia as long as they wanted to learn.

One of Hypatia's most famous students was Synesius of Cyrene, who later became the **bishop** of Ptolemais. Synesius wrote many letters, and some of them have survived to the present day. His letters to Hypatia show, long after he left Alexandria, how much he still admired his former teacher and how devoted he was to her and her teachings. In his letters,

Synesius calls Hypatia his "most reverend teacher" and a "divine spirit." α

Hypatia is believed to have written texts on subjects she had studied and mastered. By this time, she was a talented mathematician and astronomer in her own right, and she is thought to have written a commentary on *Arithmetica* by **Diophantus**, a commentary on the astronomical *Canon*, and a commentary on the *Conics* of **Apollonius**.β A commentary was an updated and revised edition of a previous work.γ

The **papyrus** scrolls in the Alexandrian libraries wore out with time and use, and they had to be recopied by hand. Scholars, like Hypatia, often revised old texts by updating them with new material and current interpretations. They made corrections and added further comments and explanations.

Hypatia may have independently revised or worked jointly with her father, Theon, on commentaries of Ptolemy's *Almagest* and *Handy Tables*.Δ These were two very important astronomical resources (and possibly part of the astronomical *Canon* mentioned earlier). In the process of restoring and updating older texts, Hypatia was preserving knowledge for future students and scholars.

Hypatia also was very knowledgeable regarding the use and construction of scientific instruments. In his letters, Synesius mentions Hypatia in relation to the astrolabe and the hydroscope.ε The astrolabe was a complicated astronomical device for determining the position of stars, planets, and other heavenly bodies. The hydroscope (hydrometer, densimeter) was an instrument for measuring the weight of liquids or for determining their relative density or specific gravity.

As a teacher, Hypatia gave lectures in her home, in lecture halls, and in public. She proved to be very popular everywhere she spoke. Her lectures were directed mainly to the upper classes of Alexandria, but at that time, teaching to any group in public was very unusual for a woman. Hypatia did it anyway. At her home, there were often crowds of people gathered and waiting to hear her speak. Public halls were frequently filled with students and officials wanting to hear her lectures.

Many of Hypatia's students went on to hold positions of authority and power across the ancient world. They became important political and religious leaders, and as a consequence, many of Hypatia's ideas and teachings became widespread. Hypatia's students did not forget their devoted teacher. Synesius, for example, said he would remember his beloved Hypatia even in **Hades**.[θ]

Hypatia was intent on passing knowledge on to her students and to preserving knowledge in general. She encouraged her students to engage in sound logic and rational thought. She wanted them to question accepted ideas, to come to their own conclusions, and to think independently. Hypatia was indeed a dedicated teacher.

Chapter 5: A Respected Philosopher

"What would you have us do, Philosopher? What will you teach us about life?"

"I hope," answered Hypatia, "to kindle within you the spark of self-exploration so that you may achieve a higher state of revelation and understanding."

Already a respected mathematician, astronomer, and scientist, Hypatia was also becoming a leading Neoplatonic **philosopher**. As a philosophy, Neoplatonism focuses on ideas about reality and truth. It is based on the teachings of **Plato** and **Plotinus**. Neoplatonism teaches that there is a supreme being or power, called the One,µ at the center of existence, and union with this being may be achieved through meditation and study.

No one is certain exactly what Hypatia taught her philosophical followers because few records survive and her select students tended to share their ideas and practices only amongst the members of their inner group. Hypatia may have encouraged her followers to look into their inner selves to examine the mystery of existence. She may have asked them to follow certain spiritual practices so they could find new meaning in their lives. By mastering self-control, eliminating worldly distractions, and following intellectual and reasoning pursuits, she may have felt they could achieve a higher state of awareness.

Following Hypatia's teachings would have required intellectual effort, will power, and moral strength. It would not have been easy. If her students succeeded in their efforts, however, they might have elevated themselves toward a higher understanding and achieved greater personal insights. They might have been able to live in harmony with themselves and follow more moral, virtuous, and ethical lives.

Hypatia spoke **articulately** and **eloquently** when she presented her philosophical lectures. She was an extremely accomplished **orator**, and both students and city leaders gathered to hear her talk. Scholars also came from distant lands to hear Hypatia speak. She used her voice to encourage **restraint** and **moderation** in life and to promote disciplined study and a love of learning.

Through her private teaching and her public lecturing, Hypatia's name became widely known. She became one of Alexandria's most admired citizens, and her fame spread beyond

Alexandria to other cities and distant lands. As a result, she attained a rather **unique** social, cultural, and political position in the city. Admired and respected by many, she was often consulted by high-ranking leaders who sought her advice on current and troubling issues. As time passed, she became more and more influential.

Socrates Scholasticus, a historian who lived around the time of Hypatia, indicated that she had:

> "made such attainments in literature and science, as to far surpass all the philosophers of her own time. Having succeeded to the school of Plato and Plotinus, she explained the principles of philosophy to her auditors, many of whom came from a distance to receive her instructions. On account of the self-possession and ease of manner, which she had acquired in consequence of the cultivation of her mind, she not unfrequently appeared in public in presence of the magistrates. Neither did she feel abashed in going to an assembly of men. For all men on account of her extraordinary dignity and virtue admired her the more." [3]

As part of the Roman Empire, Alexandria was considered a Christian city. In reality, however, many religious groups lived and worshiped there—including people of the Jewish faith and other groups who worshiped the Greek, Roman, and Egyptian gods. Other individuals did not worship any god. Although Hypatia's Neoplatonist philosophy was considered a **Pagan** philosophy, she did not worship multiple gods, and she did not engage in Pagan **cult** practices.[π] Her students and followers came from many different religious backgrounds, and her philosophical beliefs were **compatible** with many different religions.[ρ]

Religious and political conflicts, however, were increasingly playing a significant role in Alexandrian life. The city was frequently marked by various power struggles and episodes of social unrest. Many historians think the Museion and great Library had already been severely damaged by fire or completely destroyed by this time. Others believe their loss may have occurred later. In 391 CE, however, most agree that the Temple of Serapis was destroyed, and the scholarly works contained in the Serapeum were lost.

At that time, a man named Theophilus was the bishop of Alexandria. He was a powerful Christian religious leader who wanted to drive Paganism out of the city. It was Theophilus who ordered the destruction of the Serapeum and the Temple of

Serapis. He likely regarded this Pagan temple, and the scientists, mathematicians, and scholars who studied at the library, as a threat to the growth of the Christian religion. Theophilus wanted the temple gone, so he had it and the Serapeum destroyed. He replaced them with a Christian church.

Losing a wonderful library like the Serapeum was a great loss to the scholars of Alexandria, but there is no evidence Hypatia was involved in this religious **confrontation**. She continued to be a very popular and respected philosopher, orator, and teacher. Hypatia seems to have been **exempt** from the rising religious and political struggles that were occurring in the city, and she was not threatened or harmed during these increasingly **turbulent** times.$^{\Sigma}$

In 412 CE, however, Theophilus was succeeded as bishop by his nephew, Cyril. Under Cyril's leadership, the episodes of destruction and brutality between Christians and non-Christians would increase. Alexandria was rapidly becoming a city in conflict and one that was increasingly marked by social unrest, religious disagreements, and political struggles.

Chapter 6: An Unintended Martyr

"Orestes, what has happened? Blood flows from your head **profusely**."

"I believe it is Cyril, Hypatia. He has seized the **synagogues** and expelled the Jews from the city. He has called in his armed monks. They insulted me and accused me of Paganism and **idolatry**. Even when I told them I am a Christian, they would not believe me. One of them, Ammonius, threw a stone that cut my head. He tried to kill me."

"What do they hope to accomplish with such actions?"

"They are inciting **turmoil**. Their goal is power. They want to control the city. Believe me, Hypatia, Ammonius will pay for what he has done. The political and religious climate of the city is changing daily. A web of **chaos** covers Alexandria, but I will not get caught in it again."

Orestes was the civil prefect or governor of Alexandria. He, like other leaders in the city, often sought Hypatia's advice and guidance. Orestes tried to govern the city with a measure of tolerance for all of Alexandria's religious and cultural groups, but it was difficult in the confusing and uncertain times. He increasingly found himself engaged in tense power struggles with Cyril, the Christian bishop of Alexandria.

When Orestes caught Ammonius, who was one of Cyril's supporters, he had him tortured. The torture was so intense, Ammonius died. This upset Cyril greatly, and tensions rose even higher between Orestes and Cyril. These two Alexandrian leaders were in a political and religious tug-of-war for control of the city.

Although civil and religious conflicts were escalating in Alexandria, Hypatia stayed true to herself and to her beliefs. She continued to teach her students and to give her lectures. She also continued to use her voice to promote moderation in life and to encourage disciplined study.

Orestes, however, proved correct in his prediction: he did not get caught physically in the struggles again. Instead, it was Hypatia who got trapped in the web of conflict that covered the city. Few sources survive from the time period in which Hypatia lived, so it is difficult to know exactly what happened, but it is clear the winds of change were blowing in Alexandria, and they were not blowing in Hypatia's favor.

First of all, in the middle of all the political and religious fighting, some of the people in Alexandria became jealous of Hypatia's popularity and status. So many people gathered to hear her speak that some citizens and leaders felt threatened by her great influence over the city. Others were envious of Hypatia's independence, skills, **prestige**, and power.

Secondly, Hypatia was rumored to be the person responsible for preventing Orestes from settling his differences with Cyril.

Some people thought it was her fault Orestes and Cyril could not heal their wounds and work together in a peaceful manner. Rumors were spread that Hypatia was a witch. People made false claims that Hypatia had charmed Orestes with her magic, enchantments, and devilish tricks to keep him from making peace.[Φ] Most of the elite, educated people of Alexandria, who knew Hypatia, recognized that these claims were not accurate. The uneducated citizens, however, did not know Hypatia personally, and they did not understand her teachings and beliefs. Since Hypatia had little contact with the common people of Alexandria, many may have believed the lies and rumors that were spread about her.

Finally, Cyril may have turned against Hypatia because she was Orestes' friend and because she was a non-Christian. He may have felt Hypatia's philosophical and scientific ideas encouraged the very Paganism he was trying to eliminate. Many early Christians associated mathematical and scientific thought, which Hypatia represented, with Paganism. At the dangerous risk of being labeled a **heretic**, Hypatia was likely warned to stop teaching mathematics, science, and Neoplatonism.[Ψ] Staying true to her beliefs, Hypatia courageously refused and continued to teach her students. Thus, Cyril may have regarded Hypatia as a threat to the spread of Christianity. He simply may have been intimidated by her intelligence and skills, jealous of her popularity, or troubled by her relationship with Orestes. It is difficult to know for sure, but some historical sources accuse Cyril of planning Hypatia's death. Other sources indicate he was aware of a plan to attack Hypatia, but did nothing to stop it. Still others imply Cyril had nothing to do with Hypatia's death. However it happened, Hypatia's life ended abruptly and horribly.

In March of 415 CE, according to Socrates Scholasticus, Hypatia was waylaid as she was returning home, pulled from her chariot by an angry Christian mob, dragged to a church called the Caesareum, stripped naked, brutally tortured, murdered, and then her body was burned.$^{\Omega}$ Whether she died as a result of the complicated political controversies and religious conflicts that prevailed at the time or simply because some individuals were jealous of her position as a woman and envious of her skills and influence, Hypatia's life ended tragically. The people who murdered Hypatia likely did not intend for it to happen, but she became a **martyr**.

Chapter 7: A Lasting Heroine

In the late fourth century and early fifth century, Hypatia of Alexandria was one of the world's greatest mathematicians, astronomers, and philosophers. She achieved fame as an inspirational teacher, a gifted orator, and an accomplished scholar. She both challenged and transformed many of the prevailing ideas of what it was to be a female.

*At a time when many girls did not learn to read or write, Hypatia read extensively and wrote scholarly texts.

*At a time when most girls did not receive an education, Hypatia studied mathematics, science, and philosophy.

*In a time and place where the accepted goal of many young women was to be married, Hypatia chose not to marry.

*In a time and place where most women felt public life should be avoided, Hypatia became a celebrated public figure.

*In an era when most women were known only to their immediate family and close neighbors, Hypatia became a popular and recognized figure in distant lands.

*In an era when few women even considered the idea of a profession, Hypatia elected to have an academic career as a mathematician, astronomer, philosopher, teacher, and scholar.

Hypatia of Alexandria devoted her life to acquiring knowledge and seeking wisdom. She loved to learn simply for learning's sake, and she recognized the importance of preserving knowledge for future generations. Hypatia spent her life searching for truth, and in her search, she remained true to herself and to her beliefs.

The people who murdered Hypatia may have believed, with her death, that the light of her intellect and the spirit of her being would be lost forever. They may have thought she would be forgotten. It is unlikely they envisioned that Hypatia would continue to inspire people more than 1,600 years after her death. Hypatia of Alexandria has become a symbol of courage, learning, and intellectual freedom. Her light and spirit continue to shine brightly.

VOCABULARY

abstract–existing as a thought or an idea, apart from a material or concrete object

academic–a learned person, scholar, teacher

Apollonius—(*c.* 262-*c.* 190 BCE) Greek mathematician who wrote an 8-volume mathematical text called *Conics* about the geometry of cones

articulately–in a clear and understandable manner, speaking distinctly and pronouncing clearly

astronomy–study of the stars, planets, and other heavenly bodies

bishop–a high-ranking member of the Christian church

chaos–extreme confusion and great disorder

charisma–special charm, compelling attractiveness

commerce–buying and selling of goods, trade, business

compatible–in agreement, working well together

confrontation–a hostile meeting between opposing parties

cult–a system of religious beliefs, practices, and rituals; often considered to be false or extreme

Diophantus–(*c.* 214-*c.* 298 CE) Greek mathematician who wrote a 13-volume mathematical text called *Arithmetica*; he has been called the "father of algebra"

doctrines–teachings, principles, rules, policies, tenets, beliefs taught by a church

elite–superior, distinguished, powerful, upper

eloquently–in a graceful, expressive, fluent, and persuasive manner

Euclid–(*c.* 325-*c.* 265 BCE) Greek mathematician, often called the "father of geometry"

exempt–free from the conditions imposed on others, not subject to

exhilarated–elated, invigorated, stimulated, animated

fertility–producing greatly, especially producing young or crops, fruitful

geometry–branch of mathematics dealing with points, lines, and planes

grammar–the rules and correct use of a language

Hades–in Greek mythology, the underworld or underground dwelling place of the dead; a place where the spirits of the dead resided

heretic–a person who teaches or believes something at odds to the teachings and beliefs of a church

idolatry–worshipping idols or images of gods

inquisitive–asking questions, seeking information, eager to learn

martyr–a person who is killed because of their beliefs; a person who is killed because they would not renounce their faith or principles

melodic–pleasing to hear, sounding sweet, tuneful

moderation–keeping within reasonable limits, avoidance of excesses or extremes in behavior

orator–a skilled public speaker

Pagan–a person holding beliefs other than those of the main world religions; in the past, often used to indicate a non-Christian; a person who worships many different gods or entities

papyrus–type of plant found in the delta of the Nile River that was pressed and used as a writing material, paper-like material

philosopher–person who studies or is learned in a certain philosophy

Plato–(*c.* 427-*c.* 347 BCE) very influential Greek philosopher, founder of the Academy (an institution of higher learning) in Athens, studied under Socrates

Plotinus–(*c.* 205-*c.* 270 CE) leading philosopher of Neoplatonism

prestige–a high standing or reputation based on someone's character, achievements, or success; widespread admiration for achievements

profusely–in large amounts, to a great degree

Ptolemy–(*c.* 100- *c.* 170 CE) Alexandrian astronomer, mathematician, and geographer, wrote astronomical text called the *Almagest* ("the greatest work")

purity–innocence, free of sin or immorality

restraint–keeping life under control or within limits, self-control, self-discipline, moderate behavior

rhetoric–art of using words effectively

scholarly–learned, having much knowledge

scholars–learned people, specialists in an area of study

suitors–men who pursue a relationship with a woman, often with the hope of marriage

synagogues–buildings used by Jews for worship and religious study

turbulent–having confusion, conflict, and disorder, violent disturbance, agitated and unruly

turmoil–confusion, uncertainty, great disturbance

unique–unusual, special, one and only

virtue–goodness, moral excellence

DID YOU KNOW?

*The city of Alexandria was established by Alexander the Great around 331-332 BCE.

*The name Hypatia means "most high" or "supreme."

*Several essays, stories, and books have been written about Hypatia—including one work by John Toland in 1720 and another by Charles Kingsley in 1853.

*In 1893, the play, *Hypatia*, opened in London at the Haymarket Theater. It was written by G. Stuart Ogilvie.

*There is an asteroid named for Hypatia called 238 Hypatia. It was discovered by Viktor Knorre in 1884.

*Hypatia is also the name of a crater on the moon that lies along the edge of Sinus Asperitatis, a bay on the edge of Mare Tranquillitatis. It is relatively close to another crater named Theophilus.

*The Hypatia Stone is an unusual extraterrestrial rock, discovered in 1996, that contains microscopic diamonds.

*A genus of moths is named for Hypatia.

*In his 1980 book, *Cosmos*, Carl Sagan discusses Hypatia's life in Alexandria. On page 335 of this book, Sagan writes: "At a time when women had few options and were treated as property, Hypatia moved freely and unselfconsciously through traditional male domains."

*There have been scholarly journals named for Hypatia that focus on feminist studies and philosophy.

*In 2009, a movie, *Agora*, was made about Hypatia. In ancient Greece, the *agora* was an open space used for public assemblies and gatherings.

SOURCE NOTES

α "Synesius of Cyrene—Synesius' Texts," *Livius-Articles on Ancient History*. 10 August 2015. http://www.livius.org/articles/person/synesius-of-cyrene/synesius-texts/.

β Michael A. B. Deakin, *Hypatia of Alexandria: Mathematician and Martyr* (Amherst, NY: Prometheus Books, 2007), 89, 95-101, 109.

γ Margaret J. Anderson and Karen F. Stephenson, *Scientists of the Ancient World* (Berkeley Heights, NJ: Enslow Publishers, Inc., 1999), 85.

Δ Maria Dzielska, *Hypatia of Alexandria*, trans. F. Lyra (Cambridge, MA: Harvard University Press, 1995), 71-72, 102.

ε "Synesius of Cyrene—Synesius' Texts," *Livius-Articles on Ancient History*. 10 August 2015. http://www.livius.org/articles/person/synesius-of-cyrene/synesius-texts/.

θ "Synesius of Cyrene—Synesius' Texts," *Livius-Articles on Ancient History*. 10 August 2015. http://www.livius.org/articles/person/synesius-of-cyrene/synesius-texts/.

μ Deakin, *Hypatia of Alexandria: Mathematician and Martyr*, 37-39.

Ξ Socrates Scholasticus, "The Life of Hypatia," *Ecclesiastical History*, Alexandria on the Web. 22 August 2015. http://cosmopolis.com/alexandria/hypatia-bio-socrates.html.

π Dzielska, *Hypatia of Alexandria*, 83, 105.

ρ Bruce J. MacLennan, *The Wisdom of Hypatia: Ancient Spiritual Practices for a More Meaningful Life* (Woodbury, MN: Llewellyn Publications, 2013), 11.

Σ Dzielska, *Hypatia of Alexandria*, 83-84.

Φ John, Bishop of Nikiu, "The Life of Hypatia," *Chronicle* 84: 87-103. 9 August 2015. http://cosmopolis.com/alexandria/hypatia-bio-john.html.

Ψ Cynthia A. Bily, "Hypatia," in *Dictionary of World Biography: Vol. 1 The Ancient World*, ed. Frank N. Magill (Pasadena, CA: Salem Press, Inc., 1998), 437.

Ω Socrates Scholasticus, "The Life of Hypatia," *Ecclesiastical History*, Alexandria on the Web. 22 August 2015. http://cosmopolis.com/alexandria/hypatia-bio-socrates.html.

REFERENCES

Used to Tell the Story of Hypatia

Anderson, Margaret J., and Karen F. Stephenson. *Scientists of the Ancient World*. Berkeley Heights, NJ: Enslow Publishers, Inc., 1999.

Arab, Sameh M. "Bibliotheca Alexandrina: The Ancient Library of Alexandria and the Re-built of the Modern One." *Arab World Books*. Available: http://www.arabworldbooks.com/bibliothecaAlexandrina.htm.

Bily, Cynthia A. "Hypatia." In *Dictionary of World Biography: Vol. 1 The Ancient World*, ed. Frank N. Magill, 436-439. Pasadena, CA: Salem Press, Inc., 1998.

Damascius. *Life of Isidore*. "The Life of Hypatia." (Reproduced in *The Suda*) Trans. Jeremiah Reedy. Phanes Press, 1993. Available: http://www.cosmopolis.com/alexandria/hypatia-bio-suda.html.

Deakin, Michael A. B. *Hypatia of Alexandria: Mathematician and Martyr*. Amherst, NY: Prometheus Books, 2007.

Dzielska, Maria. *Hypatia of Alexandria*. Translated by F. Lyra. Cambridge, MA: Harvard University Press, 1995.

John, Bishop of Nikiu. "The Life of Hypatia." *Chronicle* 84: 87-103. Available: http://cosmopolis.com/alexandria/hypatia-bio-john.html.

MacLennan, Bruce J. *The Wisdom of Hypatia: Ancient Spiritual Practices for a More Meaningful Life*. Woodbury, MN: Llewellyn Publications, 2013.

Richeson, A. W. "Hypatia of Alexandria." *National Mathematics Magazine*. Vol. 15, No. 2 (November 1940): 74-82.

Sagan, Carl. *Cosmos*. New York, NY: Random House, Inc., 1980.

Scholasticus, Socrates. "The Life of Hypatia." *Ecclesiastical History*. Alexandria on the Web. Available: http://cosmopolis.com/alexandria/hypatia-bio-socrates.html.

"Synesius of Cyrene—Synesius' Texts." *Livius-Articles on Ancient History*. Available: http://www.livius.org/articles/person/synesius-of-cyrene/synesius-texts/.

Zielinski, Sarah. "Hypatia, Ancient Alexandria's Great Female Scholar." *Smithsonian.com*. (14 March 2010). Available: http://www.smithsonianmag.com/womens-history/hypatia-ancient-alexandrias-great-female-scholar-10942888/?all.

ADDITIONAL BOOKS YOU MAY ENJOY
by
Billie Holladay Skelley

Luella Agnes Owen: Going Where No Lady Had Gone Before
Crossing Time Series-Book 1

Ruth Law: The Queen of the Air
Crossing Time Series-Book 2

Hugh Armstrong Robinson: The Story of Flying Lucky 13
Crossing Time Series-Book 3

Hypatia: Ancient Alexandria's Female Scholar
Crossing Time Series-Book 4

Bass Reeves: Legendary Lawman of the Wild West
Crossing Time Series-Book 5

Eagle the Legal Beagle

Ollie the Autism-Support Collie

Weaver the Diabetic-Alert Retriever

Spice Secret: A Cautionary Diary

Two Terrible Days in May: The Rader Farm Massacre

It's Almost Time to Celebrate St. Patrick's Day

Tapeti: The Moon's Keeper

www.ingramcontent.com/pod-product-compliance
Lightning Source LLC
Chambersburg PA
CBHW050730010526
44107CB00009B/804